WORLD COMMODITIES

Iron Ore

GARRY CHAPMAN » GARY HODGES

This edition first published in 2011 in the United States of America by Smart Apple Media.

Smart Apple Media
P.O. Box 3263
Mankato, MN, 56002

First published in 2010 by
MACMILLAN EDUCATION AUSTRALIA PTY LTD
15–19 Claremont Street, South Yarra 3141

Visit our web site at www.macmillan.com.au or go directly to www.macmillanlibrary.com.au

Associated companies and representatives throughout the world.

Library of Congress Cataloging-in-Publication Data

Chapman, Garry.
  Iron ore / Garry Chapman and Gary Hodges.
     p. cm. — (World commodities)
  Includes index.
  ISBN 978-1-59920-585-4 (library binding)
  1. Iron industry and trade—Juvenile literature. 2. Iron ores—Juvenile literature. 3. Iron—Juvenile literature. I. Hodges, Gary. II. Title.
  HD9510.5.C42 2011
  338.2'73—dc22
                              2010007307

Publisher: Carmel Heron   Designer: Ivan Finnegan (cover and text)
Commissioning Editor: Niki Horin   Page Layout: Ivan Finnegan
Managing Editor: Vanessa Lanaway   Photo Researcher: Lesya Bryndzia (management: Debbie Gallagher)
Editor: Laura Jeanne Gobal   Illustrators: Andy Craig and Nives Porcellato, 15; Alan Laver, 17
Proofreader: Kirstie Innes-Will   Production Controller: Vanessa Johnson

Manufactured in the United States of America by Corporate Graphics, Minnesota.
052010

Acknowledgments

The author and the publisher are grateful to the following for permission to reproduce copyright material:

Front cover photograph of iron ore mining: 123RF/Zavalnyuk Sergey

The Art Archive/Museum of London, 8; Bloomberg via Getty Images/Pauline Bax, 10 (top), /Carla Gottgens 11 (middle); Corbis/Australian Picture Library/Chris Boydell, 10 (bottom), /Barnabas Bosshart, 22, /EPA/Franck Robichon, 21, /Karen Kasmauski, 11 (bottom right), /Charles O'Rear, 10 (middle left), /Redlink, 20; Getty Images/AFP/Tony McDonough, 19, /Sean Gallup, 28, /Peter Hendrie, 24, 25, /Dorling Kindersley, 4 (iron ore), /National Geographic/James L. Amos, 11 (bottom left), /National Geographic/Emory Kristof, 11 (top right), /John Wildgoose, 18; table information supplied by ISSB Ltd, 16; iStockphoto/Adam Goldsmith, 9 (bottom), /mikeuk, 7, /Joerg Reimann, 26; Newspix/Angelo Soulas, 11 (top right); LKAB, 29; Photolibrary/Neil Duncan, 27, /Peter Arnold Images/Jim Wark, 23, /Jose Fuste Raga, 9 (top), /Schiller Schiller, 12 (top); Shutterstock/Antikainen, 12 (middle), /Forest Badger, 4 (oil), /Elena Elisseeva, 13, /hainaultphoto, 14, /IDAL, 4 (wheat), /SergioZ, 12 (bottom), /June Marie Sobrito, 5, /Worldpics, 4 (coal), /yykkaa, 4 (sugar), /Magdalena Zurawska, 4 (coffee).

While every care has been taken to trace and acknowledge copyright, the publisher tenders their apologies for any accidental infringement where copyright has proved untraceable. Where the attempt has been unsuccessful, the publisher welcomes information that would redress the situation.

Please note: At the time of printing, the Internet addresses appearing in this book were correct. Owing to the dynamic nature of the Internet, however, we cannot guarantee that all of these addresses will remain correct.

This series is for my father, Ron Chapman, with gratitude. – Garry Chapman
This series is dedicated to the memory of Jean and Alex Ross, as well as my immediate family of Sue, Hannah and Jessica, my parents, Jim and Val, and my brother Leigh. – Gary Hodges

Contents

Glossary Words

When a word is printed in **bold**, you can look up its meaning in the Glossary on page 31.

What Is a World Commodity?

A commodity is any product for which someone is willing to pay money. A world commodity is a product that is traded across the world.

The World's Most Widely Traded Commodities

Many of the world's most widely traded commodities are **agricultural** products, such as coffee, sugar, and wheat, or **natural resources**, such as coal, iron ore, and oil. These commodities are produced in large amounts by people around the world.

Coal, coffee, iron ore, oil, sugar, and wheat are important commodities traded around the world.

Commodities and the World's Economy

Whenever the world's **demand** for a commodity increases or decreases, the price of this commodity goes up or down by the same amount everywhere. Prices usually vary from day to day. The daily trade in world commodities plays a key role in the state of the world's **economy**.

MORE ABOUT...
The Quality of Commodities

When people, businesses or countries buy a commodity, they assume that its quality will be consistent. Oil is an example of a commodity. When people trade in oil, all barrels of oil are considered to be of the same quality regardless of where they come from.

Iron Ore is a Commodity

Iron ore is a natural resource used in the manufacture of iron and steel—the world's most commonly used metals.

An Abundant Mineral

Iron ore is the most abundant mineral on Earth. It makes up about 5 percent of Earth's crust and an even higher percentage of Earth's inner core. Iron ore is a combination of iron and oxygen, also known as iron oxide. To obtain iron, the oxygen has to be removed from the ore, which is found in rocks.

Iron ore is used to make steel, which, in turn, is used to make many large structures, such as this steel footbridge.

Types of Iron Ore

The most common types of iron ore are hematite and magnetite. Hematite is 70 percent pure iron, while magnetite is 72 percent pure iron.

Iron Alloys

Iron is often combined with other metals to form **alloys**. Alloys have many positive attributes, including strength, resistance to wear, springiness, and the ability to keep a sharp edge. Steel is an alloy. It is used mainly in the construction of buildings, bridges, ships, and vehicles. It is also used to make many household items.

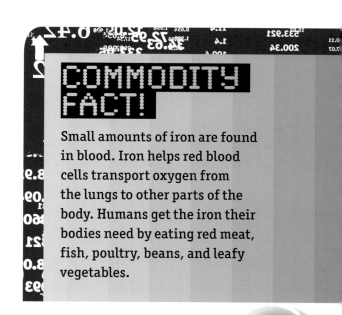

COMMODITY FACT!

Small amounts of iron are found in blood. Iron helps red blood cells transport oxygen from the lungs to other parts of the body. Humans get the iron their bodies need by eating red meat, fish, poultry, beans, and leafy vegetables.

Where Is Iron Ore Found and Where Is It Used?

Iron ore is found throughout the world. However, not all iron-rich rocks can be mined and transported easily. This is why some countries dominate the iron-ore trade.

Major Producers of Iron Ore

China produces more iron ore than any other country. Its largest mine, at Benxi, produces hematite and magnetite. Although a major producer of iron ore, each year China must also **import** a large amount of iron ore to meet its growing demand. Brazil, the second-largest producer of iron ore, mines mainly magnetite and Australia, the third-largest producer, mines mainly hematite.

Hematite

Hematite is the main ore used in the production of iron and steel. Hematite is found in banded iron formations, which consist of thin layers of iron oxides alternating with other types of rock. The Pilbara region of Western Australia is a major producer of hematite.

Magnetite

Magnetite has a lower iron content than hematite and is also low in impurities. This makes it useful when producing steel with a low level of impurities. Large amounts of magnetite can be found in **sedimentary** banded-iron formations and also in sand. Large magnetite deposits are mined in Brazil, Australia, India, and the United States.

THE WORLD'S MAJOR PRODUCERS OF IRON ORE (2008)

Country	Amount of Iron Ore Produced
China	403 million tons (366 million t)
Brazil	381 million tons (346 million t)
Australia	374 million tons (340 million t)
India	235 million tons (214 million t)
Russia	110 million tons (100 million t)

Growing World Consumption

World consumption of iron ore is growing rapidly and increasing at a significant rate each year. This is largely due to the **economic boom** in **developing countries**, such as China and India, and their subsequent need for steel for construction. The global demand for iron ore is expected to remain quite high for some time.

This hematite has formed in layers of orange and black, giving it the nickname "tiger iron."

The Big Consumers

China is currently the world's largest consumer of iron ore as it produces more steel annually than any other country. Other major consumers of iron ore include Japan and South Korea. Unable to produce enough iron ore to meet their huge demands, these countries import large amounts of iron ore from other parts of the world.

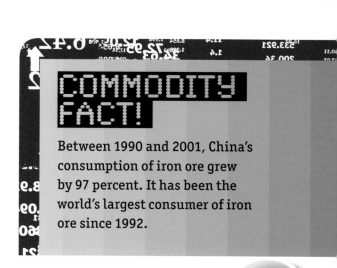

COMMODITY FACT!

Between 1990 and 2001, China's consumption of iron ore grew by 97 percent. It has been the world's largest consumer of iron ore since 1992.

Timeline: **The History of Iron Ore**

Iron ore is of little or no use in its pure form. For this reason, the history of iron ore is closely linked to the invention and development of blast furnaces, which **smelt** the ore to create **pig iron**.

2500 B.C.
The earliest iron implements are produced in the Middle East by smelting iron ore in a bloomery, a type of furnace.

about 100
The blast furnace is developed in China during the Han Dynasty. The pig iron it produces is used to make tools and weapons of **wrought iron** and steel.

1491
Blast furnaces are introduced to England from Normandy, France. They use charcoal for fuel.

Roman daggers were made of steel, which is made from iron ore.

2500 B.C.

400
In Europe, the Romans, Greeks, and Celts use bloomeries. Roman soldiers carry weapons made of steel.

about 1450
Bloomery and osmond iron-making processes are gradually replaced by finery processes. In a finery **forge**, pig iron is made into **bar iron**.

1620
The British iron industry reaches its peak and starts a slow decline until the early 1700s. This is because it is cheaper for the British to import iron from Sweden.

550
The Chinese make farm tools and weapons from **cast iron**.

A.D. 1150
Europe's first blast furnaces are built in Switzerland, Germany, and Sweden between 1150 and 1350. The Swedes produce balls of wrought iron, known as osmonds, which are traded across borders.

1709
Abraham Darby begins fuelling a blast furnace with **coke** (made from coal) instead of charcoal. This produces higher-quality iron at a lower cost.

1770s

The Industrial Revolution, a period of time when manufacturing by machines in factories grew in importance and scale, begins. Wrought iron is used in the construction of steam engines, train engines, and ships. Bridges, aqueducts, and canals made of cast iron are erected.

1856

Henry Bessemer invents a new steel-making process, which produces larger amounts of **mild steel** at a cheaper price. Mild steel soon replaces wrought iron in manufacturing.

The Iron Bridge in Shropshire, England, was the world's first cast-iron bridge. It was built in the 1770s.

1828

James Beaumont Neilson improves the steel-making process by preheating the blast. This reduces the cost of producing steel.

1950s

The basic oxygen process of steel making is introduced, rapidly converting several hundred tons of iron into steel. Most steel is now made this way.

1960s

Plastics begin to replace steel in many products.

A.D. 2010

1846

The cast-iron Dee Bridge in Cheshire, England, collapses when the weight of a train causes a beam to bend at its center. Many similar bridges are demolished and rebuilt with wrought iron.

1925

James Aston develops a process for mass-producing wrought iron quickly and at a low cost.

2010

Iron ore continues to play an important role in the global economy, especially in developing countries, such as China and India. China's steel industry is now the biggest consumer of iron ore in the world.

1879

The cast-iron Tay Bridge, connecting the city of Dundee and the town of Wormit in Scotland, collapses. Thousands of other cast-iron rail bridges are replaced with steel bridges.

1784

Henry Cort invents the puddling furnace, which produces iron with fewer impurities.

During the Industrial Revolution, steam engines were constructed from wrought iron.

How Is Iron Ore Mined?

Like most minerals, iron ore is found beneath the ground. This means it has to be dug out and sent to a factory, where it can be processed into useful materials.

Exploration

Mining companies send exploration teams into regions where iron ore is likely to be found. The teams gather rock samples and analyze them.

Surveys and Feasibility Studies

If iron ore is present, the area is surveyed to determine the extent of the ore deposits and their likely commercial value. If high-grade ore is found in large amounts, a study is conducted to determine whether a mining operation will be successful. A mine will be set up only if the study indicates that the mine will be profitable.

Establishing a Mine Site

Mine buildings and processing plants are then built. Roads and railways are constructed to transport mined ore to the nearest port or steelworks.

Mining Operations

Mining operations begin. The mining company will recover iron ore from the mine until it is no longer profitable to do so.

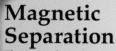

Waste Storage

The waste is called mullock. Mullock is stored in waste dumps until the mine is closed. It is then used to fill up the large mining holes during **land reclamation**.

Magnetic Separation

The powdered ore and rock are passed beneath a magnetic separator, which attracts iron ore particles and leaves everything else behind as waste. The finely crushed ore is then stored. It will be sent to a steelworks.

Land Reclamation

Once mining operations have ceased, the mining company helps to reclaim the land. This involves restoring the landscape, planting trees, and reintroducing **native** wildlife to the area.

Crushing and Grinding

The boulders are coarsely crushed, then washed to separate smaller rocks and lighter soil from the heavier ore. The ore is then crushed and ground, resulting in a fine mix of powdered ore and rock.

Excavation

Explosives are placed in holes which have been drilled into the mine floor. The blasts from the explosion create massive boulders. These are scooped up by large bulldozers, loaded into big trucks, and transported to a crushing plant.

Producing Iron and Steel

Once iron ore has been crushed and waste material removed, it is ready to be made into iron or steel through smelting.

Fueling the Blast Furnace

Iron ore, coke, and limestone are fed into the top of a furnace. A blast of heated air is fed into the bottom of the furnace. The temperature inside the blast furnace will reach around 3,632 degrees°F (2,000 degrees°C).

Inside the Blast Furnace

Coke reacts with oxygen in the blast of air and forms carbon monoxide. The carbon monoxide causes the iron ore to change into molten iron. The limestone melts the impurities present in the iron ore and forms **slag**, which floats to the top of the molten iron. The slag and the molten iron flow out of separate openings on the side of the furnace.

Pig Iron

The metal cools and solidifies to form pig iron and the slag is removed.

Turning Pig Iron into Steel

Pig iron has a high percentage of carbon and other impurities. Carbon makes the pig iron brittle and hard. To remove the carbon, the pig iron is heated in another furnace with oxygen. Oxygen combines with some of the carbon and impurities, and removes them from the pig iron to form steel. The higher the amount of remaining carbon, the harder the steel will be. When the steel is heated and then cooled in water, it becomes less brittle.

Most of today's cooking pots and pans are made from stainless steel, which is an alloy made from pig iron and chromium.

Steel Alloys

Different types of steel can be obtained by adding small amounts of other metals to pig iron. This creates **alloys**, which are usually costlier to produce than regular steel. Chromium is added to make stainless steel. Other metals used to make alloys include molybdenum, vanadium, nickel, and tungsten.

COMMODITY FACT!

Iron can withstand very high temperatures. A skilful **blacksmith** can form just about any shape imaginable from heated iron using simple tools, such as a hammer and anvil. When cooled, the shape becomes permanent.

The Iron Ore Trade

Iron ore is the commodity we rely on when strong building materials are needed for the construction of skyscrapers, factories, stadiums, bridges, and other structures. This makes iron ore a very valuable trade commodity.

Direct Deals

Iron ore is traded in a slightly different way from other commodities, which are usually traded through exchanges, or commodities markets. Rather than buying and selling through exchanges or other trade agencies, large mining companies and iron and steel manufacturers tend to deal with each other directly.

Setting a Benchmark Price

At the end of each year, high-volume iron-ore transactions occur between mining companies and iron and steel manufacturers. When a fair price has been negotiated between them, it becomes the benchmark, or standard price, for all iron ore transactions in the following year.

Steel is used in the construction of skyscrapers, such as the Burj Khalifa in the United Arab Emirates. It is the world's tallest building.

COMMODITY FACT!

China dominates the iron-ore trade, consuming more than 50 percent of the total iron-ore produced. In 2009, China imported 630 million tons (570 million t) of iron ore!

Moving Toward the Spot Market

In recent years, there have been moves toward using the spot market for negotiations and setting iron-ore prices. In the spot market, buyers and sellers agree on a price for the immediate exchange of goods. This means iron ore is delivered to the buyer as soon as it is purchased.

The problem with the benchmark system is that it protects steelmakers, but not mining companies. When spot prices are higher than the benchmark, some steelmakers use the lower benchmark price and save money on their purchase. When spot prices are lower than the benchmark, some steelmakers ignore the benchmark and instead trade on the spot market in order to pay lower prices.

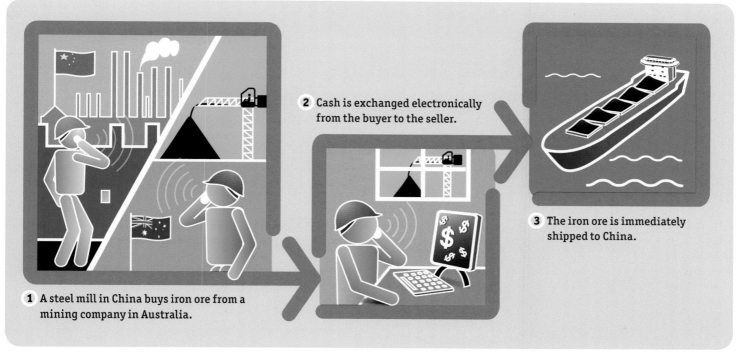

2 Cash is exchanged electronically from the buyer to the seller.

3 The iron ore is immediately shipped to China.

1 A steel mill in China buys iron ore from a mining company in Australia.

The spot trading of iron ore is a simple transaction between a mining company and a steel mill that takes place in three main stages.

Transportation Costs

Spot prices usually reflect the cost of transporting iron ore from where it was mined to where it will be processed. If the ore has to travel long distances, transportation costs will be high and the trade will be less profitable.

Supply and Demand

The iron ore trade is determined by **supply** and demand. When consumers are eager to buy the commodity, the demand for iron ore increases. Consumers rely on producers to supply it.

Factors Affecting Supply

The supply of iron ore is heavily influenced by demand for the commodity. It can also be influenced by factors such as the discovery of new ore deposits, technological advances in mining techniques, and the ability of ports to manage the transportation and storage of iron ore. Changes related to any of these factors can have an impact on the ability of iron-ore producers to meet the demands of consumers.

Factors Affecting Demand

The demand for iron ore is usually affected by the pace of global economic activity. During an economic downturn, countries tend to cut back on imports. A fall in demand for cars and building materials, for example, would mean there is less demand for steel, and therefore less demand for iron ore. As a result, the price may also fall. The **export** earnings of countries that supply iron ore will fall too.

THE WORLD'S TOP EXPORTERS AND IMPORTERS OF IRON ORE (2008)

Exporter	Amount of Iron Ore Exported	Importer	Amount of Iron Ore Imported
Australia	339,823,805 tons (308,930,732 t)	China	488,431,009 tons (444,028,190 t)
Brazil	309,850,950 tons (281,682,682 t)	Japan	154,386,393 tons (140,351,266 t)
India	67,490,147 tons (61,354,679 t)	South Korea	54,496,501 tons (49,542,274 t)
South Africa	34,751,152 tons (31,591,956 t)	Germany	49,929,967 tons (45,390,879 t)
Canada	30,861,102 tons (28,055,547 t)	Netherlands	35,906,913 tons (32,642,648 t)

Price Variations

The price of iron ore is subject to variations, just like the prices of other commodities, which are influenced by supply and demand. However, iron-ore price variations tend to be from year to year and are announced by the trading parties concerned, once an agreement has been reached.

THE RISE AND FALL OF THE WORLD PRICE OF IRON ORE

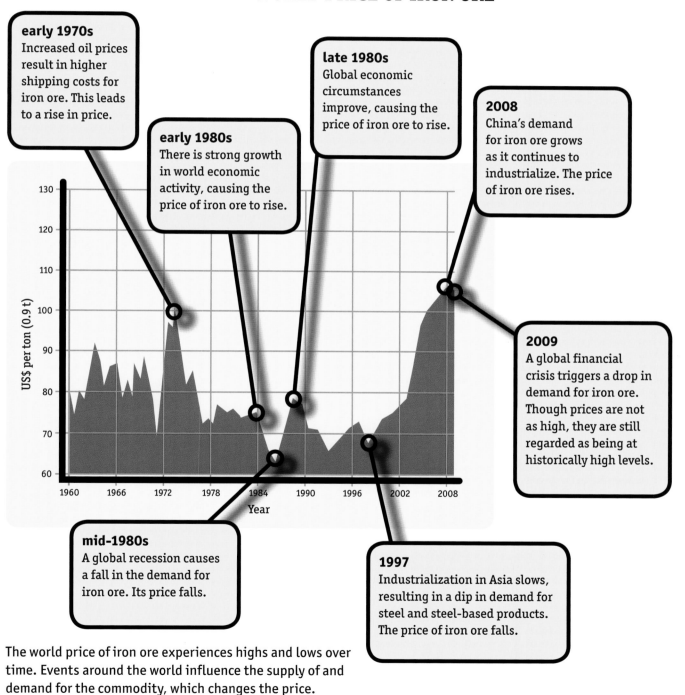

early 1970s
Increased oil prices result in higher shipping costs for iron ore. This leads to a rise in price.

early 1980s
There is strong growth in world economic activity, causing the price of iron ore to rise.

late 1980s
Global economic circumstances improve, causing the price of iron ore to rise.

2008
China's demand for iron ore grows as it continues to industrialize. The price of iron ore rises.

2009
A global financial crisis triggers a drop in demand for iron ore. Though prices are not as high, they are still regarded as being at historically high levels.

mid-1980s
A global recession causes a fall in the demand for iron ore. Its price falls.

1997
Industrialization in Asia slows, resulting in a dip in demand for steel and steel-based products. The price of iron ore falls.

The world price of iron ore experiences highs and lows over time. Events around the world influence the supply of and demand for the commodity, which changes the price.

Codes of Practice

Codes of practice govern the way most commodities are traded internationally. The purpose of these codes is to ensure that commodities are fairly priced and traded. However, iron-ore trades proceed without the involvement of any kind of industry association or global **regulator**.

Controlling the Market

A small number of the world's largest mining companies control the price and the amount of iron ore produced. This can make it difficult for smaller producers to enter the trading market. Buyers end up having to pay a higher price than they would if there were more competition in the market. There have been very few attempts at regulating the iron-ore market and it seems unlikely that any future attempts will succeed.

Negotiations between large mining companies and steel manufacturers can take several months.

Contract Negotiations

The iron-ore trade involves billions of dollars and the transport of thousands of tons of ore. This means contract negotiations, particularly those which set the benchmark price, can take time. Talks begin toward the end of December and agreement may not be reached until July of the following year. In such situations, smaller producers may turn to the regulated framework of the spot market for a price instead of waiting for the benchmark to be set by the largest mining companies.

The Big Players

Anglo-Australian mining companies BHP Billiton and Rio Tinto, together with Brazil's Vale, are the world's major iron-ore mining companies. In recent times, these companies have negotiated profitable contracts to sell iron ore to China's giant Baoshan Iron & Steel Company (Baosteel). Since 2006, Baosteel has been responsible for negotiating iron-ore deals on behalf of China's steelworks.

Rio Tinto, one of the largest mining companies in the world, has facilities in Kwinana, Western Australia. The facilities were visited by Chinese Premier Wen Jiabao in 2006.

COMMODITY FACT!

In 2009, China set up the Rizhao International Iron Ore Trade Center. It provides a range of services for the two parties involved in any iron-ore trade, including inspection of the ore, storage, transportation, and insurance. The center promotes orderly iron-ore imports and standardizes the way in which buyers and sellers conduct business.

International Politics and Iron Ore

Many international companies and their governments rely on the iron-ore trade for healthy national economies. This trade involves billions of dollars and thousands of tons of ore changing hands around the world every year.

A High-pressure Industry

Export earnings are very important to a country's economy, its development, and its standing in the international trading community. Export earnings are also very important to the mining companies, which need good profits to keep their investors happy. This places enormous pressure on everyone involved in the iron-ore trade.

Ore-consuming Countries

The iron and steel manufacturers of ore-consuming countries negotiate iron-ore prices with mining companies. The outcome of these international negotiations has an enormous impact on **domestic** iron and steel industries. If prices are reasonable, good profits can be made. Steelworkers are likely to benefit from this by earning higher wages. Governments are also likely to benefit by receiving more income from taxes. Both the manufacturers and the producers aim to get the best deal, and sometimes this can lead to disputes between countries.

Up to 110,000 tons (100,000 t) of steel, all made in China, was used to construct the Beijing National Stadium. It is the world's largest steel structure, built to host the 2008 Olympic Games.

Japan

Japanese steel manufacturers have had to pay high prices for iron ore from the world's largest mining companies. This has been reflected in higher prices for Japanese electronic goods and vehicles. Such prices have weakened Japan's competitiveness in the international **consumer goods** market. As it becomes harder for Japanese companies to sell their products internationally, greater pressure is placed on steel manufacturers and the government to negotiate better deals in order to protect their economy.

Japan exports millions of cars to countries around the world. However, the high price of iron ore means that its car industry is not as competitive in the international market.

China

In 2009, negotiations between China and mining companies Rio Tinto, BHP Billiton and Vale broke down as a result of China wanting an almost 50 percent drop in prices from 2008 levels. The mining companies would not agree to this because they had already negotiated a 33 percent reduction with Japan and South Korea. The situation worsened quickly and, in March 2010, executives from Rio Tinto were found guilty of bribery and obtaining secret company information.

Some experts believe China needs to negotiate a benchmark price that benefits its steel mills because it is the world's largest consumer of iron ore. It cannot rely on the spot market because spot prices have increased dramatically. As for the mining companies, it is important that they maintain a good relationship with China, because of China's position in the market.

Environmental Issues and Iron Ore

Developing countries, such as China and India, rely heavily on access to steel for the construction of factories, buildings, bridges, cars, and railways. This creates a huge demand for iron ore and also creates challenges for the environment.

What are the Environmental Issues?

Some of the environmental issues that accompany iron-ore mining are:

- limiting dust pollution to keep the environment and people in it safe
- removing and later replacing of soil
- logging and revegetating of forested areas
- minimizing the disruption to surrounding **ecosystems**, particularly to vulnerable plants and animals
- disposing safely of mining waste products

"Mining takes place in all countries. There is a huge demand for steel and this is met by mining iron ore. The arguments against mining are flawed. Instead there should be a strong demand for **sustainable** *mining."*

Sujay Gupta, Vice President of Communications, Sociedade de Fomento
(Source: www.corpwatch.org/article.php?id=15351)

Destruction of the Landscape

Mining operations can cause great damage to the landscape. Rocks and soil are removed during mining operations and forests are cleared, greatly disturbing ecosystems. Mining companies must take responsibility for restoring the land to its original state once mines are closed.

The mining of iron ore creates a lot of dust. Special vehicles spray water on the roads to reduce the amount of dust in the air.

Air Pollution

Open-pit mining operations generate a lot of dust. Blasts from explosives and the removal of rocks and soil can stir up thick clouds of fine dust particles. Large amounts of dust can affect plants in the area by limiting the amount of sunlight they receive. Dust is also a health concern for humans. Many mining companies take action to minimize dust pollution.

MORE ABOUT...
Water Pollution in Goa

Goa, on India's west coast, is famous for its beaches. Goa is also located close to about 100 iron-ore mines. Some of the area's rivers no longer flow and wells have run dry. They are filled with red mud, carelessly dumped by irresponsible mining companies. Whether the waterways can be saved is unknown.

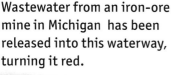

Wastewater from an iron-ore mine in Michigan has been released into this waterway, turning it red.

Problems with Waterways

Mining operations may also result in changes to the natural flow of waterways and drainage systems. Underground water reserves, known as aquifers, also might be affected, particularly those which are found near iron-ore deposits or those into which mining waste flows. Mining companies must ensure that no harmful changes to water systems occur as a result of their operations.

Social Issues and Iron Ore

Social issues related to iron-ore mining are usually connected to providing support to old and new communities affected by iron-ore mines.

Creating a New Community

Mines are usually found in areas far away from established towns and cities. When a new mine is set up, a new town is often set up, too. Such towns are built to house mine workers and their families, and provide the facilities that all families need, including stores, schools, healthcare, and entertainment.

Port Hedland, in Australia, and its surrounding towns were built to support Australia's iron-ore trade.

Looking after an Existing Community

If a mine site is set up near an existing town, mining companies must make connections with the local community. While a mine is in operation, many community members will probably be employed within the mining industry or its support services, such as transportation or food supply. The mine will depend on the community, and the community will depend on the mine.

Keeping the Community Safe

Health and safety issues must also be addressed when setting up a new mine site. Mining companies must keep dust to a minimum by covering the beds of iron-ore trucks with tarpaulins and spraying water on mine roads. They must also reduce noise levels from the mine and ensure that any wastewater recycled for the community is clean.

Planning for the Future

When the mine is about to close, it is important that mining companies help prepare their workers by retraining them for other work or by helping them to find work in other mines. Mining companies also can support the development of agriculture or other industries in the region to ensure employment opportunities for their workers.

Accommodations and many other facilities must be built for mine workers and their families in a new town.

Is the Iron Ore Industry Sustainable?

To sustain something is to keep it going for a very long time. There are two main aspects to keeping the iron ore industry sustainable: maintaining the demand for iron ore and protecting the environment from the effects of mining iron ore.

A Nonrenewable Resource

Iron ore is readily available around the world and will be for a long time. However, iron ore is a **nonrenewable** resource, and a time will come when it can no longer be relied on. It is unlikely that the demand for iron and steel will fall greatly, due to its importance in the construction and transportation industries, or that alternatives to steel will be introduced. Therefore, we must find a way to make the steel we have last as long as possible. The best way to do this is to recycle.

Cars contain a lot of steel, which can be recycled by a junk yard when the car is no longer used.

COMMODITY FACT!

Steel is now the most recycled material on Earth. In 2008, 83.3 percent of all the world's scrap steel was recycled. Not only does this reduce the cost of new steel, it also prevents the original steel materials from being disposed of in landfills.

Recycling

Much of the iron and steel we no longer use can be recycled. Steel food cans, for example, can be recycled cheaply and easily without affecting the metal's physical properties. Recycling will ensure that iron and steel will be available for hundreds of years. It will also ease the pressure on Earth's precious natural resources. Recycling also means the environment will be less affected by mining operations.

Protecting the Environment

Mining companies have a responsibility to return mined land to its natural state. There are a number of ways they can do this.

- They can refill mining pits with soil and rocks, which were removed during the mining process.
- They can replant trees and vegetation to encourage native wildlife to return to the former mine site.
- They can stock large water storages at the mine site with fish or transform them into reservoirs to provide water for local farms.
- They can help streams and other waterways to flow naturally again.

By taking care of the environment, mining companies can help ensure the sustainability of ecosystems.

Replanting vegetation is one way of reclaiming a mine site. Here, a man sows grass seeds at an old mine.

The Future of the Iron Ore Industry

The future of iron ore as a commodity seems bright, particularly since estimates suggest that iron-ore reserves should last for another 100 years. With new and improved mining techniques and the cooperation of ore producers and mining companies, the iron-ore industry will remain strong.

China's Growing Demand

China is the world's leading consumer of iron ore. This consumption is expected to grow in the future. However, China's domestic iron ore is being depleted, so it has to depend on imports. How long China can continue its extraordinary growth is one of the main issues facing the iron-ore industry. Without China's demand, it is possible that the industry will decline. However, based on the number and size of the blast furnaces that are planned in China, the iron-ore industry should continue to grow.

Joining Forces

It seems likely that the world's three major iron-ore producers (BHP Billiton, Rio Tinto, and Vale) will continue to export large amounts of iron ore to China, India, Japan, and South Korea well into the future. Industry observers expect to see these and other companies join forces and work together on particular aspects of the mining process as well. Such cooperation could help reduce costs and boost profits.

Large iron-ore reserves mean that steel manufacturers will have plenty of raw materials to work with in the future.

Automated Mining

Rio Tinto and the U.S. technology company General Electric (GE) have been discussing plans to automate future mine-to-port operations. Some of the features of this initiative include energy-efficient and driverless trains and trucks, along with remote-controlled intelligent drills. The mine of the future could even be remotely controlled from a distance!

In the future, iron-ore mining may involve remote-controlled operations, making it safer.

Recycling

One of the biggest advantages of the iron and steel industry is that iron and steel can be recycled. This means that even if iron-ore reserves are depleted in the future, we will be able to control our use of iron ore by recycling unwanted steel products. The iron ore reserves that remain can then be saved for the most important uses.

Find Out More

Web Sites for Further Information

- ### Different types of iron ore
  Learn more about the different types of iron ore and their properties.
  www.mii.org/Minerals/photoiron.html

- ### How are iron and steel made?
  Learn more about the properties of iron and steel and how they are made.
  http://science.howstuffworks.com/iron.htm

- ### How is stainless steel made?
  Learn more about the manufacture of stainless steel.
  www.madehow.com/Volume-1/Stainless-Steel.html

- ### BHP Billiton's iron-ore production
  Learn more about one of the world's largest iron-ore mining companies.
  www.bhpbilliton.com.au/bb/ourBusinesses/ironOre.jsp

Focus Questions

These questions might help you think about some of the issues raised in this book.

- What are the reasons for China's growing need for iron ore?

- What are some possible reasons for buyers and sellers of iron ore to deal with each other directly rather than trade on commodities exchanges?

- Is having a few large companies dominating the iron-ore trade good for the industry?

- Does our demand for products containing steel guarantee a promising future for the iron-ore trade?

Glossary

agricultural	related to farming or used for farming
alloys	metals made from a mixture of one metal with another metal or with a nonmetal
bar iron	iron in the form of bars that can be beaten into a range of shapes by a blacksmith
blacksmith	someone who makes things from iron
cast iron	a type of hard iron that does not bend easily
coke	a solid material made from coal and burned to make steel
consumer goods	goods that are produced for the use of individuals rather than for the production of other goods
demand	the amount of a product consumers want to buy
developing countries	countries in the early stages of becoming industrialized
domestic	relating to a person's own country
economic boom	a time when an economy is growing rapidly
economy	a system that organizes the production, distribution, and exchange of goods and services, as well as incomes
ecosystems	communities of plants and animals that interact with one another and with the environments in which they live
export	a product which is sold to another country; or the action of sending a product to another country to sell it
forge	the place where a metal is heated before it is shaped
import	a product which is bought or brought in from another country; or the action of buying and bringing a product into a country
land reclamation	the restoration of an area, such as a mine site, to its natural state
mild steel	a commonly used form of steel that is very strong
native	grows naturally in an area
natural resources	the naturally occurring, useful wealth of a region or country, such as land, forests, coal, oil, gas, and water
nonrenewable	from a source that will run out
pig iron	an impure form of iron
regulator	someone or something that makes sure that companies in the same industry work in a fair and effective way
sedimentary	made by the deposit of sediments, which are small pieces of solid material
slag	a waste product that forms when metal is removed from its ore
smelt	to extract metal from rock by heating it to a very high temperature
supply	the amount of a product that producers are able to sell
sustainable	developed or designed so that the production of a commodity can continue for a long time
wrought iron	iron which is almost free of carbon

Index